The Bible: What's in It for Me?

A four-week course to help adults discover exciting biblical truths for everyday living.

by
Stephen Parolini

Apply·It·To·Life™

Adult

BIBLE CURRICULUM
from Group

Group
Loveland, Colorado

Apply·It·To·Life™
Adult
BIBLE CURRICULUM

Group

The Bible: What's in It for Me?
Copyright © 1995 Group Publishing, Inc.

Credits
Editor: Michael Warden
Senior Editor: Paul Woods
Creative Products Director: Joani Schultz
Cover Designer: Liz Howe
Interior Designer: Kathy Benson
Illustrator: Rex Bohn
Cover Illustrator: Walter Stanford; The Stock Illustration Source, Inc.
ISBN 1-55945-504-7

10 9 8 7 6 5 4 3 2 1   04 03 02 01 00 99 98 97 96 95

Printed in the United States of America.

C O N T E N T S

Getting to Know God
We can get to know God through Bible study.

Our Questions, God's Answers
Wisdom from the Bible is valuable in our lives.

A Relationship Blueprint
The Bible provides a blueprint for relationships with other people and
with God.

Exploring the Bible in Context
If we study the context of a Bible passage, we can better understand
and apply the passage.

Introduction

WHAT IS APPLY-IT-TO-LIFE™ ADULT BIBLE CURRICULUM?

Apply-It-To-Life™ Adult Bible Curriculum is a series of four-week study courses designed to help you facilitate powerful lessons that will help adults grow in faith. Use this course with

- Sunday school classes,
- home study groups,
- weekday Bible study groups,
- men's Bible studies,
- women's Bible studies, and
- family classes.

The variety of courses gives the adult student a broad coverage of topical, life-related issues and significant biblical topics. In addition, as the name of the series implies, every lesson helps the adult student apply Scripture to his or her life.

Each course in Apply-It-To-Life Adult Bible Curriculum provides four lessons on different aspects of one topic. In each course, you also receive Fellowship and Outreach Specials connected to the month's topic. They provide suggestions for building closer relationships in your class, outreach activities, and even a party idea!

WHAT MAKES APPLY-IT-TO-LIFE ADULT BIBLE CURRICULUM UNIQUE?

Teaching as Jesus Taught

Jesus was a master teacher. With Apply-It-To-Life Adult Bible Curriculum, you'll use the same teaching methods and principles that Jesus used:

- **Active Learning.** Think back on an important lesson you've learned in life. Did you learn it from reading about it? from hearing about it? from something you did? Chances are, the most important lessons you've learned came from something you experienced. That's what active learning is—learning by doing. Active learning leads students through activities and experiences that help them understand important principles, messages, and ideas. It's a discovery process that helps people internalize and remember what they learn.

Jesus often used active learning. One of the most vivid examples is his washing of his disciples' feet. In Apply-It-To-Life Adult Bible Curriculum, the teacher might remove his or her shoes and socks then read aloud the foot-washing passage from John 13, or the teacher might choose to actually wash people's feet. Participants won't soon forget it. Active learning uses simple activities to teach profound lessons.

● **Interactive Learning.** Interactive learning means learning through small-group interaction and discussion. While it may seem to be a simple concept, it's radically new to many churches that have stuck with a lecture format or large-group discussion for so long. With interactive learning, each person is actively involved in discovering God's truth through talking with other people about God's Word. Interactive learning is discussion with a difference. It puts people in pairs, trios, or foursomes to involve everyone in the learning experience. It takes active learning a step further by having people who have gone through an experience teach others what they've learned.

Jesus often helped cement the learning from an experience by questioning people—sometimes in small groups—about what had happened. He regularly questioned his followers and his opponents, forcing them to think and to discuss among themselves what he was teaching them. After washing his disciples' feet, the first thing Jesus did was ask the disciples if they understood what he had done. After the "foot washing" activity, the teacher might form small groups and have people discuss how they felt when the leader removed his or her shoes and socks. Then group members could compare those feelings and the learning involved to what the disciples must have experienced.

● **Biblical Depth.** Apply-It-To-Life Adult Bible Curriculum recognizes that most adults are ready to go below the surface to better understand the deeper truths of the Bible. Therefore, the activities and studies go beyond an "easy answer" approach to Christian education and lead adults to grapple with difficult issues from a biblical perspective.

Each lesson begins by giving the teacher resource material on the Bible passages covered in the study. In the Bible Basis, you'll find information that will help you understand the Scriptures you're dealing with. Within the class-time section of the lesson, thought-provoking activities and discussions lead adults to new depths of biblical understanding. Bible Insights within the lesson give pertinent information that will bring the

Bible to life for you and your class members. In-class handouts give adults significant Bible information and challenge them to search for and discover biblical truths for themselves. Finally, the "For Even Deeper Discussion" sections provide questions that will lead your class members to new and deeper levels of insight and application.

No one questions the depth of Jesus' teachings or the effectiveness of his teaching methods. This curriculum follows Jesus' example and helps people probe the depths of the Bible in a way no other adult curriculum does.

● **Bible Application.** Jesus didn't stop with helping people understand truth. For him, teaching took the learner beyond understanding to application. It wasn't enough that the rich young ruler knew all the right answers. Jesus wanted him to take action on what he knew. In the same way, Apply-It-To-Life Adult Bible Curriculum encourages a response in people's lives. That's why this curriculum is called "Apply-It-To-Life"! Depth of understanding means little if the truths of Scripture don't zing into people's hearts. Each lesson brings home one point and encourages people to consider the changes they might make in response.

● **One Purpose.** In each study, every activity works toward communicating and applying the same point. People may discover other new truths, but the study doesn't load them down with a mass of information. Sometimes less is more. When lessons try to teach too much, they often fail to teach anything. Even Jesus limited his teaching to what he felt people could really learn and apply (John 16:12). Apply-It-To-Life Adult Bible Curriculum makes sure that class members thoroughly understand and apply one point each week.

● **Variety.** People appreciate variety. Jesus constantly varied his teaching methods. One day he would have a serious discussion with his disciples about who he was and another day he'd baffle them by turning water into wine. What he didn't do was allow them to become bored with what he had to teach them.

Any kind of study can become less than exciting if the leader and students do everything the same way week after week. Apply-It-To-Life Adult Bible Curriculum varies activities and approaches to keep everyone's interest level high each week. In one class, you might have people in small groups "put themselves in the disciples' sandals" and experience something of the confusion of Jesus' death and resurrection. In another lesson, class members may experience problems in communication and examine how such problems can damage relationships.

To meet adults' varied needs, the courses cover a wide range of topics such as Jesus, knowing God's will, communication, taking faith to work, and highlights of Bible books. One month you may choose to study a family or personal faith issue; the next month you may cover a biblical topic such as the book of John.

● **Relevance.** People today want to know how to live successfully right now. They struggle with living as authentic Christians at work, in the family, and in the community. Most churchgoing adults want to learn about the Bible, but not merely for the sake of having greater Bible knowledge. They want to know how the Bible can help them live faithful lives—how it can help them face the difficulties of living in today's culture. Apply-It-To-Life Adult Bible Curriculum bridges the gap between biblical truth and the "real world" issues of people's lives. Jesus didn't discuss with his followers the eschatological significance of Ezekiel's wheels, and Apply-It-To-Life Adult Bible Curriculum won't either! Courses and studies in this curriculum focus on the real needs of people and help them discover answers in Scripture that will help meet those needs.

● **A Nonthreatening Atmosphere.** In many adult classes, people feel intimidated because they're new Christians or because they don't have the Bible knowledge they think they should have. Jesus sometimes intimidated those who opposed him, but he consistently treated his followers with understanding and respect. We want people in church to experience the same understanding and respect Jesus' followers experienced. With Apply-It-To-Life Adult Bible Curriculum, no one is embarrassed for not knowing or understanding as much as someone else. In fact, the interactive learning process minimizes the differences between those with vast Bible knowledge and those with little Bible knowledge. Lessons often begin with nonthreatening, sharing questions and move slowly toward more depth. Whatever their level of knowledge or commitment, class members will work together to discover biblical truths that can affect their lives.

● **A Group That Cares.** Jesus began his ministry by choosing a group of 12 people who learned from him together. That group practically lived together—sharing one another's hurts, joys, and ambitions. Sometimes Jesus divided the 12 into smaller groups and worked with just three or four at a time.

Studies have shown that many adults today long for a close-knit group of people with whom they can share personal needs and joys. And people interact more freely when they feel accepted in a group. Activities in this curriculum will help class members get to know one another better and care for one another more as they study the Bible and apply its truths to their lives. As people reveal their thoughts and feelings to one another, they'll grow closer and develop more commitment to the group and to each other. And they'll be encouraging one another along the way!

● **An Element of Delight.** We don't often think about Jesus' ministry in this way, but there certainly were times he brought fun and delight to his followers. Remember the time he raised Peter's mother-in-law? or the time he sat happily with children on his lap? How about the joy and excitement at his triumphal entry into Jerusalem? or the time he helped fishing disciples catch a boatload of fish—after they'd fished all night with no success?

People learn more when they're having fun. So within Apply-It-To-Life Adult Bible Curriculum, elements of fun and delight pop up often. And sometimes adding fun is as simple as using a carrot for a pretend microphone!

Taking the Fear out of Teaching

Teachers love Apply-It-To-Life Adult Bible Curriculum because it makes teaching much less stressful. Lessons in this curriculum

● **are easy to teach.** Interactive learning frees the teacher from being a dispenser of information to serve as a facilitator of learning. Teachers can spend class time guiding people to discover and apply biblical truths. The studies provide clear, understandable Bible background; easy-to-prepare learning experiences; and powerful, thought-provoking discussion questions.

● **can be prepared quickly.** Lessons in Apply-It-To-Life Adult Bible Curriculum are logical and clear. There's no sorting through tons of information to figure out the lesson. In 30 minutes, a busy teacher can easily read a lesson and prepare to teach it. In addition, optional and For Extra Time activities allow the teacher to tailor the lesson to the class. And the thorough instructions and questions will guide even an inexperienced teacher through each powerful lesson.

● **let everyone share in the class's success.** With Apply-It-To-Life Bible Curriculum, the teacher is one of the participants. The teacher still guides the class, but the burden is not as heavy. Everyone participates and adds to the study's effectiveness. So when the study has an impact, everyone shares in that success.

● **lead the teacher to new discoveries.** Each lesson is designed to help the teacher first discover a biblical truth. And most teachers will make additional discoveries as they prepare each lesson. In class, the teacher will discover even more as other adults share what they have found. As with any type of teaching, the teacher will likely learn more than anyone else in the class!

● **provide relevant information to class members.**

Photocopiable handouts are designed to help people better understand or interpret Bible passages. And the handouts make teaching easier because the teacher can often refer to them for small-group discussion questions and instructions.

HOW TO USE APPLY-IT-TO-LIFE ADULT BIBLE CURRICULUM

First familiarize yourself with an Apply-It-To-Life Adult Bible Curriculum lesson. The following explanations will help you understand how the lesson elements work together.

Lesson Elements

● The **Opening** maps out the lesson's agenda and introduces your class to the topic for the session. Sometimes this activity will help people get better acquainted as they begin to explore the topic together.

● The **Bible Exploration and Application** activities will help people discover what the Bible says about the topic and how the lesson's point applies to their lives. In these varied activities, class members find answers to the "So what?" question. Through active and interactive learning methods, people will discover the relevance of the Scriptures and commit to growing closer to God.

You may use either one or both of the options in this section. They are designed to stand alone or to work together. Both present the same point in different ways. "For Even Deeper Discussion" questions appear at the end of each activity in this section. Use these questions whenever you feel they might be particularly helpful for your class.

● The **Closing** pulls everything in the lesson together and often funnels the lesson's message into a time of reflection and prayer.

● The **For Extra Time** section is just that. Use it when you've completed the lesson and still have time left or when you've used one Bible Exploration and Application option and don't have time to do the other. Or you might plan to use it instead of another option.

When you put all the sections together, you get a lesson that's fun and easy to teach. Plus, participants will learn truths they'll remember and apply to their daily lives.

About the Questions and Answers . . .

The answers given after discussion questions are responses participants *might* give. They aren't the only answers or the "right" answers. However, you can use them to spark discussion.

Real life doesn't always allow us to give the "right" answers. That's why some of the responses given are negative or controversial. If someone responds negatively, don't be shocked. Accept the person and use the opportunity to explore other perspectives on the issue.

To get more out of your discussions, use follow-up inquiries such as

- Tell me more.
- What do you mean by that?
- What makes you feel that way?

Guidelines for a Successful Adult Class

- **Be a facilitator, not a lecturer.** Apply-It-To-Life Adult Bible Curriculum is student-based rather than teacher-based. Your job is to direct the activities and facilitate the discussions. You become a choreographer of sorts: someone who gets everyone else involved in the discussion and keeps the discussion on track.

- **Teach adults how to form small groups.** Help adults discover the benefits of small-group discussions by assisting them in forming groups of four, three, or two—whatever the activity calls for. Small-group sharing allows for more discussion and involvement by all participants. It's not as threatening or scary to open up to two people as it would be to 20 or 200!

Some leaders decide not to form small groups because they want to hear everybody's ideas. The intention is good, but some people just won't talk in a large group. Use a "report back" time after small-group discussions to gather the best responses from all groups.

When you form small groups, don't always let people choose those right around them. Try creative group-forming methods to help everyone in the class get to know one another. For example, tell class members: find three other people wearing the same color you are; join two other people who like the same music you do; locate three others who shop at the same grocery store you do; find one who was born the same month as you; choose three who like the same season as you, and so on. If you have fun with it, your class will, too!

● **Encourage relationship building.** George Barna, in his insightful book about the church, *The Frog in the Kettle,* explains that adults today have a strong need to develop friendships. In a society of high-tech toys, "personal" computers, and lonely commutes, people long for positive human contact. That's where our church classes and groups can jump in. Help adults form friendships through your class. What's discovered in a classroom setting will be better applied when friends support each other outside the classroom. In fact, the relationships begun in your class may be as important as the truths you help your adults learn.

● **Be flexible.** Sometimes your class will complete every activity in the lesson with great success and wonderful learning. But what should you do if people go off on a tangent? or they get stuck in one of the activities? What if you don't have time to finish the lesson?

Don't panic. People learn best when they are interested and engaged in meaningful discussion, when they move at their own pace. And if you get through even one activity, your class will discover the point for the whole lesson. So relax. It's OK if you don't get everything done. Try to get to the Closing in every lesson, since its purpose is to bring closure to the topic for the week. But if you don't, don't sweat it!

● **Expect the unexpected.** Active learning is an adventure that doesn't always take you where you think you're going. Don't be surprised if things don't go exactly the way you'd planned. Be open to the different directions the Holy Spirit may lead your class. When something goes wrong or an unexpected emotion is aroused, take advantage of this teachable moment. Ask probing questions; follow up on someone's deep need or concern. Those moments are often the best opportunities for learning that come our way.

● **Participate—and encourage participation.** Apply-It-To-Life Adult Bible Curriculum is only as interactive as you and your class make it. Learning arises out of dialogue. People need to grapple with and verbalize their questions and discoveries. Jump into discussions yourself, but don't "take over." Encourage everyone to participate. You can facilitate smooth discussions by using "active listening" responses such as rephrasing and summing up what's been said. If people seem stumped, use the possible responses after each question to spark further discussion. You may feel like a cheerleader at times, but your efforts will be worth it. The more people participate, the more they'll discover God's truths for themselves.

● **Trust the Holy Spirit.** All the previous six guidelines and the instructions in the lessons will be irrelevant if you ignore the presence of God in your classroom. God sent the Holy Spirit as our helper. As you use this curriculum, ask the Holy Spirit to help you facilitate the lessons. And ask the Holy Spirit to direct your class toward God's truth. Trust that God's Spirit can work through each person's discoveries, not just the teacher's.

How to Use This Course

Before the Four-Week Session
● Read the Course Introduction and This Course at a Glance (pp. 13-14).

● Decide how you'll use the art on the Publicity Page (p. 15) to publicize the course. Prepare fliers, newsletter articles, and posters as needed.

● Look at the Fellowship and Outreach Specials (pp. 63-64) and decide which ones you'll use.

Before Each Lesson
● Read the one-sentence Point, the Objectives, and the Bible Basis for the lesson. The Bible Basis provides background information on the lesson's passages and shows how those passages relate to people today.

● Choose which activities you'll use from the lesson. Remember, it's not important to do every activity. Pick the ones that best fit your group and time allotment.

● Gather necessary supplies. They're listed in "This Lesson at a Glance."

● Read each section of the lesson. Adjust activities as necessary to fit your class size and meeting room, but be careful not to delete all the activity. People learn best when they're actively involved in the learning process.

COURSE INTRODUCTION: THE BIBLE: WHAT'S IN IT FOR ME?

While respect for the Bible is declining in our society, Christians are rediscovering their need to learn more about it. This course is designed to help people discover new relevance in the Bible and learn how to apply the teachings we find in its God-inspired words.

Christians disagree about many details of God's revealed truth in the Bible, but we can all agree that God wants us to explore his Word. Through this course, people will dive into the Bible in many different ways—and begin to apply the richness of wisdom that lies within it.

Bible study isn't always easy. It involves more than flipping through the pages and finding a verse or two to

● Seventy-seven percent of Christians say they're interested or very interested in studying the Bible.

● Only 32 percent of Americans today believe the Bible is true (as opposed to 65 percent in the 1960s).

soothe a troubled mind. Yet solid Bible study is essential to understanding the God who calls us into a relationship with him and with his people. And we need to study and understand biblical truths before they can begin to make a difference in our lives.

Take up the challenge of God's Word with your class and see what new insights you discover. With the Holy Spirit to guide you, these next four weeks will be full of exciting twists, turns, and opportunities to grow closer to God and closer together as followers of Jesus.

This Course at a Glance

Before you dive into the lessons, familiarize yourself with each lesson's point. Then read the Scripture passages.

- Study them as a background to the lessons.
- Use them as a basis for your personal devotions.
- Think about how they relate to people's situations today.

Lesson 1: Getting to Know God
The Point: We can get to know God through Bible study.
Bible Basis: Psalm 119:1-16 and Colossians 3:15-17

Lesson 2: Our Questions, God's Answers
The Point: Wisdom from the Bible is valuable in our lives.
Bible Basis: Psalm 19:7-11; Proverbs 2:1-6; Acts 17:11-12; and 2 Timothy 3:16-17

Lesson 3: A Relationship Blueprint
The Point: The Bible provides a blueprint for relationships with other people and with God.
Bible Basis: 1 John 4:19-21 and Luke 11:37-54

Lesson 4: Exploring the Bible in Context
The Point: If we study the context of a Bible passage, we can better understand and apply the passage.
Bible Basis: 1 Peter

Grab your congregation's attention! Add the vital details to the ready-made flier below, photocopy it, and use it to advertise this course on applying the Bible to our lives. Insert the flier in your bulletins. Enlarge it to make posters. Splash the art or anything else from this page in newsletters, bulletins, or even on postcards! It's that simple.

The art from this page is also available on Group's MinistryNet™ computer on-line resource for you to manipulate on your computer. Call 800-447-1070 for information.

The Bible: What's in It for Me?

A four-week adult course on applying the Bible to life.

COME TO

ON

AT

Come learn how the Bible can strengthen your relationship with God and with others.

The Bible: What's in It for Me?

The Bible: What's in It for Me?

The Bible: What's in It for Me?

The Bible: What's in It for Me?

Getting to Know God

We can get to know God through Bible study.

◀ **THE POINT**

OBJECTIVES

Participants will
- discover how we learn about God through the Bible,
- learn the value of studying the Bible, and
- commit to study the Bible during the coming week.

BIBLE BASIS

Read the Scripture for this lesson. Then read the following background paragraphs to see how the passages relate to people today.

In **Psalm 119:1-16,** the psalmist praises God's Word. This familiar passage is often used as a biblical basis for Scripture memorization (as implied by some translations which read, "hidden your word in my heart"). It also gives us the Bible's best description of the beauty and value of God's Word.

PSALM 119:1-16

Psalm 119 is the longest of all the Psalms, and also displays the most intricate construction. It's like a giant acrostic! A successive letter of the Hebrew alphabet labels each of the 22 eight-verse sections, using all 22 Hebrew letters. Also, within each section, each of the eight verses begins with the Hebrew letter that labels the section. Because of the psalm's intricacy, most scholars conclude that this psalm, unlike most others, was not to be sung. The writer likely intended that people read Psalm 119 carefully and meditatively.

Throughout this Psalm, the psalmist emphasizes love and respect for God and Scripture. The writer uses eight different Hebrew words in describing God's Word, and every section contains at least six of them. In fact, almost all verses contain at least one of those words.

In spite of all the structure and repetition, Psalm 119 isn't a dry, lifeless monologue. Instead, it's a powerful outpouring from the author's heart. With great care, thought, and emotion, the psalmist expressed his passion for knowing God through his Word.

Sometimes we study the Bible just because we think we should or because we feel guilty if we don't. Or we choose to study the Bible because we're looking for an answer to a specific problem. The psalmist suggests that we study the Bible to better understand and know God—and live godly lives.

COLOSSIANS 3:15-17

In **Colossians 3:15-17,** Paul tells his readers to let the word of Christ dwell in them.

Based upon Paul's letter to the Colossians, it appears that many people in Colossae were following the teachings of a heresy called Gnosticism. In this false belief, people claimed to have special intellectual knowledge of spiritual things—an elite knowledge that the masses would never be able to attain. Part of that "special knowledge"—at least in Corinth—was the belief that Jesus was inferior to God the Father and even to the angels.

Paul counters this heresy with a powerful and clear theology explaining Jesus' existence as God from eternity past. Paul knew that the Christians in Colossae would be better prepared to reject false doctrines such as Gnosticism if they were well-instructed in the doctrine of Christ.

Today false doctrines abound, and Paul's encouragement to the Colossian Christians applies to us, too. By studying the truth about Jesus, we'll get to know God better. We'll also be better prepared to turn away from or dismiss the false doctrines that clutter *our* world. And what's our best resource for learning about Jesus? You guessed it—the Bible.

Jesus knew the Old Testament well, and he used Scripture to deal with many difficult situations. We, too, can learn to study the Bible and apply it to life. Though finding a time for Bible study isn't always easy in today's so-much-to-do/so-little-time society, it's vital to daily Christian living. Diving into God's Word can be the most rewarding and valuable thing we do.

Section	Minutes	What Participants Will Do	Supplies
OPENING	*up to 10*	**BEST BIBLE STORIES**—Learn about today's lesson and tell each other what Bible stories they remember from childhood.	
BIBLE EXPLORATION AND APPLICATION	*20 to 30*	☐ *Option 1:* **WHAT CAN WE LEARN**—Learn about each other based on the contents of their wallets or purses, then read Hebrews 1:1-2 and discuss how we learn about God.	Bibles
	15 to 20	☐ *Option 2:* **WHY STUDY?**—Examine Psalm 119:1-16 and Colossians 3:15-17 to discover biblical reasons for studying the Bible.	Bibles, "Investigative Reports" handouts (p. 25)
CLOSING	*up to 5*	**THE BEAUTIFUL WORD**—Commit to study the Bible this week.	Bibles
⏱ **FOR EXTRA TIME**	*up to 10*	**IF WE DIDN'T HAVE THE BIBLE . . .**—Discuss what the world would be like without the Bible.	
	up to 10	**WHICH BIBLE?**—Compare various Bible translations.	Bibles

Best Bible Stories

(up to 10 minutes)

Open with a prayer of thanks for those who attended class today.

As you begin the class, form groups of four. Encourage class members to get together with people they don't know well. Have the person in each foursome who's owned his or her Bible the longest begin by telling the group members what his or her favorite Bible story was as a child. If people don't have early childhood experience with the Bible, let them tell about their earliest exposures to the Bible and what affected them most.

After class members tell about their favorite Bible stories, ask the following questions. Allow group discussion after each question before asking volunteers to share their group's ideas with the whole class. Ask:

● **What makes a Bible story popular with children?** (It's full of action; it has a nice ending.)

● **As a child, what did you think of the Bible?** (That it was boring; that it was for adults; that it had lots of interesting stories.)

● **How does our view of the Bible change as we grow older?** (The Bible becomes more complex; we try to get more out of the Bible; we're often challenged when we study the Bible.)

Say: **Children often view the Bible with awe. And they hunger for more wonderful stories of God's actions in the world. But as we grow older, that sense of wonder can become a sense of frustration or guilt when we neglect to study the Bible as much as we feel we should. During this course, we're going to explore how we can regain a wonder and hunger for the Word of God. One thing that will help us in regaining that hunger is to remember that ▶ the Bible helps us to know God.**

THE POINT ▷

Encourage class members to get involved in the discussions and activities during the study.

☐ **OPTION 1:**

What Can We Learn?

(20 to 30 minutes)

Have each foursome arrange itself into a small circle. Tell people to introduce themselves by name only. Then say: **We're going to learn a bit more about each other through a** simple exercise. **Beginning with the person in your group who's been at our church the longest, pull at least six different items from your pockets, purse, or billfold for all group members to see. Coins or multiples of any other item count as only one piece. Display the items in front of you.**

Allow two or three minutes for group members to silently examine the items other group members have displayed.

Then have people tell what they assume about each other based on the items displayed. For example, someone might say "You seem to be interested in sports because you have a ticket to a basketball game" or "You're very proud of your family because you carry lots of their pictures." Tell people to neither confirm nor deny assumptions during this time.

Allow about five minutes for people to share their thoughts. When time is up, have group members let each other know which assumptions were accurate and which weren't.

Give people about five minutes to discuss the following questions within their groups. Then ask volunteers to share their groups' insights with the whole class.

Ask:

● **What did you learn about each other from this activity?** Answers will vary.

● **What was it like to assume things about someone by looking at the items from his or her pocket, wallet or purse?** (I was pleased at what I discovered; I felt uncomfortable making guesses about them.)

● **How do we assume things about God when studying the Bible?** (We learn what God is like from what we see in his Word; Sometimes I'm not sure if I understand him right.)

Say: **Let's take a look at a passage that tells us how we learn about God from the Bible.**

In their groups, have people read Hebrews 1:1-2 and discuss the following questions. Ask:

● **What does this passage tell us about how we get to know God?** (We learn about him from the prophets and Jesus; He has revealed himself to us through the Bible.)

● **How is the way you discovered things about each other similar to the way we discover things about God from the Bible?** (We learn by looking at the things that represent people and God; we learn about God through bits and pieces of information he reveals to us.)

Have groups report their discoveries, then say: **Getting to know God through the Bible is an adventure. Sometimes we read things that surprise us. Sometimes we discover that our assumptions were right after all. But we can be sure that the Bible is**

Allow people to select items they feel comfortable showing to others. Suggest things such as keys, photographs, candy wrappers, ticket stubs, drivers' licenses.

our best source for learning about God. And with the help of the Holy Spirit, ▷ we can get to know God through the Bible.

■ ■

FOR *Even Deeper*
DISCUSSION

Form groups of no more than four and discuss the following questions:

● What can we learn about God from sources other than the Bible? Explain.

● How do we know that the Bible is reliable? that it provides an accurate picture of God?

● How can we defend the authority of the Bible to people who don't accept it as truth?

■ ■

BIBLE
INSIGHT

In Psalm 119, the author uses eight different Hebrew words in referring to God's message given to humans. These eight words are translated by nine different English words in the New International Version: law, laws, statutes, precepts, commands, commandments, decrees, word, promise. The psalmist uses these words in two ways, describing God's Word as both guidelines and promises for our lives.

BIBLE
INSIGHT

When Paul speaks of "the word of Christ" in Colossians 3:16, he's referring to the teachings of Jesus which were being orally transmitted since the gospels were not yet written. Also, many of the "psalms, hymns, and spiritual songs" had been written to preserve essential doctrines of Jesus' teachings. To sing them was to recall and rejoice in what Jesus had said and done.

☐ OPTION 2:
Why Study?
(15 to 20 minutes)

Form groups of no more than four. Assign half of the groups Psalm 119:1-16 and the other half Colossians 3:15-17.

Distribute pencils and copies of the "Investigative Reports" handout to all class members. Say: **You are now staff members of the "Investigative Reports" news show. You want to examine why Christians are so interested in studying the Bible. In your group, choose someone to fill each role listed on the handout. Spend the next 10 minutes reading your assigned passage and discussing it from the viewpoint of your particular character. Use the questions on your handout to guide your study. Discover all you can from your passage that relates to reasons for studying the Bible. You may need to read verses that precede or follow your assigned passage to help uncover the context of the message.**

While people are reading and discussing their Scripture passages, visit the groups and add your own insights to their discussions. Encourage everyone to stay focused on the task and to spend the entire time exhausting ideas about what the passages say about Bible study.

After 10 minutes, call time and say: **Before we look at what you discovered, let's talk about the experience of studying the Bible together.**

Have volunteers from each group answer the following questions. Make sure each group member has a chance to answer at least one question.

Ask:

● **What was it like to spend 10 minutes exploring one passage?** (We could've used more time; we didn't know what to say after two minutes.)

● **What was the easiest thing about examining these passages?** (They seemed pretty clear; they weren't very long.)

● **What does this experience say about Bible study?** (It takes work; it's not always easy; it can be fun.)

Have reporters from each group tell what they discovered during their study time. Encourage discussion from other groups if they agree or disagree with a group's findings.

After people have discussed each others' reports, ask:

● **Now what would you say this experience tells us about studying the Bible?** (Many insights can come out of the same passage; studying with friends can help.)

● **How are the messages of these passages relevant to us today?** (Studying the Bible is important to having the best life possible; if we're going to tell others about Christ, we must know God's Word.)

● **How does studying the Bible help us get to know God?** (We learn about him because the Bible is his message to us; he reveals himself to us through his Word.)

Say: **During the next three weeks, we'll explore different ways to discover practical applications of biblical truths. Through our studies, ▶we'll see how helpful the Bible can be in getting to know God.**

T E A C H E R

TIP

Encourage people to be honest about their feelings and to speak up even if they disagree with someone's insight. Some of the best learning and insight grows out of honest dialogue.

◀ **THE POINT**

■■■■■■■■■■■■■■■■■■■■■■■■■■

FOR *Even Deeper*
DISCUSSION

Form groups of no more than four and discuss the following questions:

● As a goal of Bible study, how important is gaining Bible knowledge? discovering applications for your situation? making changes in your life in response to what you learn?

● How do Christians today tend to rationalize away things the Bible says? How can we avoid falling into that kind of rationalization?

■■■■■■■■■■■■■■■■■■■■■■■■■■

APPLY▪IT▪TO
LIFE
THIS WEEK

The "Apply-It-To-Life This Week" handout helps people further explore the issues uncovered in today's class. Give everyone a photocopy of the handout (p. 26). Encourage class members to take time during the coming week to explore the questions and activities listed on the handout.

The Beautiful Word

(up to 5 minutes)

Say: **By studying only a few small Bible passages, as we did today, we still got to know God better. We discovered that** **God wants us to study the Bible so we can learn more about him and how to live Christlike lives. But we need to ask ourselves one more question: What am I going to do about it? Whenever we study the Bible and see that we can apply it to our lives, we need to decide what action we're going to take.**

This week, let's apply our discoveries to our daily lives and commit to study the passages on our "Apply-It-To-Life This Week" handout. Each day let's examine the passage listed and see what it teaches us about studying God's Word. As we pray, make your own commitment to God to study his Word this week.

Wrap up today's study with a creative prayer. Have volunteers take turns completing the following statement, "Dear God, your Word is like..." with a positive word or phrase, then have the whole class repeat "Help us study the Bible more so that we get to know you better."

⏱ For Extra Time

IF WE DIDN'T HAVE THE BIBLE...

(up to 10 minutes)

Form pairs and have partners take turns completing the following sentence as many ways as they can: If we didn't have the Bible...

Encourage pairs to think of as many ideas as possible. When you have just a couple of minutes left in class, call time and have a volunteer from each pair share one sentence completion with the whole class.

WHICH BIBLE?

(up to 10 minutes)

Have volunteers with different versions of the Bible read select passages to compare the translations. Have people discuss why they read a particular version of the Bible or what they'd like to know about Bible translations. If this generates a lot of interest among class members, consider having your pastor talk to your group about the strengths of each translation.

INVESTIGATIVE REPORTS

1. Within your group, choose a different person to fill each of the following roles so that every person has a role.

ROLES:

Researcher—Read the passage aloud and lead the group in searching for information about studying the Bible.

Creative Director—Help research the passage, and work to come up with creative ways to present what you've found.

Producer—Help research the passage, make final decisions about what to report, and write up what the reporter will say to the class.

Reporter—Help research the passage, and be ready to report to the class what your group discovers.

2. As you study within your group, refer to the following information related to your passage.

Psalm 119:1-16—In Psalm 119, the author uses eight different Hebrew words in referring to God's message given to humans. These eight words are translated by nine different English words in the New International Version: law, laws, statutes, precepts, commands, commandments, decrees, word, promise. The psalmist uses these words in two ways, describing God's Word as both guidelines and promises for our lives.

Colossians 3:16—When Paul speaks of "the word of Christ," he is referring to the teachings of Jesus, which were being orally transmitted since the gospels were not yet written. Also, many of the "psalms, hymns, and spiritual songs" had been written to preserve essential doctrines of Jesus' teachings. To sing them was to recall and rejoice in what Jesus had said and done.

3. Use the following questions to help you examine your passage.

What does it say? (Summarize the passage.)

What does it mean? (Determine what you think the author was trying to communicate.)

How does it apply to our lives? (Consider what application the verses have for people today.)

Getting to Know God

The Point: ▶ We can get to know God through Bible study.
Scripture Focus: Psalm 119:1-16 and Colossians 3:15-17

Reflecting on God's Word

Each day this week, read one of the following Scriptures and examine what that passage says about God's Word. List your discoveries in the space under each passage.

Day 1: Matthew 7:28-29. Jesus teaches with authority.

Day 2: James 1:22. James connects knowledge with obedience.

Day 3: Matthew 13:53-57. Jesus is not accepted in his own hometown.

Day 4: Matthew 22:23-33. Jesus speaks of knowing Scripture.

Day 5: Luke 24:44-49. Jesus points out prophecies about himself.

Day 6: 2 Timothy 3:14-17. Paul talks of the importance of Scripture.

Beyond Reflection

1. Visit your church's library or a local Christian bookstore and find a Bible commentary. Look up a few favorite passages and compare the commentator's insights with your own for those passages.

2. Meet with a friend over coffee and discuss creative ways to do Bible study. Brainstorm practical methods for spending time either together or alone in Bible study. Avoid choosing methods that might be too tough to follow through on. Start with something you see as do-able. Even a little Bible study is better than none.

3. Read a few paragraphs from a favorite book (other than the Bible). Study that passage to see what you can learn about the story, the characters, the setting, the conflict, and even the author. Then use the same technique on a passage of Scripture. Use this experience to determine how you might best study the Bible.

Next Week's Bible Passages: Psalm 19:7-11; Proverbs 2:1-6; Acts 17:11-12; and 2 Timothy 3:16-17

Our Questions, God's Answers

Wisdom from the Bible is valuable in our lives.

◀ THE POINT

OBJECTIVES

Participants will
- examine what the Bible says about wisdom,
- discover how the Bible can provide wisdom for living, and
- ask God to direct them to help them seek and apply biblical wisdom in their lives.

BIBLE BASIS

Look up the following Scriptures. Then read the background paragraphs to see how the passages relate to adults today.

Psalm 19 begins with David praising God for his glory revealed in creation. To the Israelites, "El," the name David uses for God in Psalm19:1, declared God's power and glory in nature. Then, in **Psalm 19:7-11,** David uses "LORD," a more personal name for God—one that the Israelites saw as declaring God's counsel and will through Scripture. David uses this name for God to introduce a new topic: the magnificence and value of God's Word.

PSALM 19:7-11

Throughout this passage, David names more and more benefits of living by God's Word, using different words to represent different aspects of the Word and our obedience to it.

PROVERBS 2:1-6

ACTS 17:11-12

2 TIMOTHY 3:16-17

In **Proverbs 2:1-6,** the writer intertwines the promises related to wisdom with the conditions for receiving it. He points out that wisdom doesn't just come automatically, but that we need to seek it and ask God for it. Only then will we receive wisdom, knowledge, and understanding from the Lord.

Proverbs 2:5 begins to sum up the verses preceding it. In this verse, "the fear of the Lord" doesn't involve fear as we normally think of it, but refers to appropriate reverence and worship to God. So this verse says that if we seek God's wisdom sincerely and carefully, we'll not only gain wisdom, but we'll understand God better and revere him more.

In Proverbs 2:6, the writer concludes these verses by telling us that wisdom, knowledge, and understanding come from God. And God communicates wisdom, knowledge, and understanding to us through his Word.

In **Acts 17:11-12** the Bereans receive Paul's message eagerly, but test it against the Scriptures.

Paul's preaching in Berea was primarily to Jews. These Jews may have heard of Jesus, but they apparently had never heard the full message of Jesus.

The message that Paul preached to the Bereans was the same message he had preached to the Thessalonians a few days earlier. He explained to them, using the Old Testament Scriptures, that the messiah they had been waiting for had to suffer and rise from the dead. Then he proclaimed to them that Jesus was that messiah (Acts 17:2-3; for a more complete example of Paul's message, see Acts 13:16-41).

The Bereans did three good things in this incident: they listened to Paul with open minds; they checked Paul's message against Scripture to see if it was true; and upon discovering the truth, they accepted it wholeheartedly. They were neither too skeptical to consider the message of Christ nor too naive to accept any message without checking it against God's Word.

In **2 Timothy 3:16-17,** Paul explains the importance of Scripture and the authority behind it.

In reporting that all Scripture is inspired by God ("God-breathed" in the New International Version), Paul doesn't explain exactly what that means. However, that term powerfully emphasizes the authority of the Old Testament Scriptures. If God inspired (or breathed) the Old Testament in some way, it has to be reliable. And from other passages (1 Timothy 5:18 and 2 Peter 3:15-16) we can deduce that New Testament—though some books in it had not yet been written—carries that same authority.

Because of its authority, Paul declares the Bible useful in four areas. In the area of *teaching,* it provides all anyone needs to learn about eternal life through faith in Jesus (see

2 Timothy 3:15). When it comes to *identifying error,* the Bible gives us all the information we need to refute any lie about Christianity. As for *correcting,* we can use Scripture to help restore someone who has fallen away from the faith. And for *training in righteousness,* nothing anywhere can better guide a child or an adult toward favor with God than God's own Word.

As hard as some scholars have tried to discredit the Bible, it still proves true and reliable. It speaks with God's authority and provides powerful wisdom for living faithful lives. We couldn't ask for a more valuable source to guide us day by day in our walk with God.

THIS LESSON AT A GLANCE

Section	Minutes	What Participants Will Do	Supplies
OPENING	up to 10	**WISDOM FROM ABOVE**—Discuss their study of the Bible through the week and learn about today's lesson.	
BIBLE EXPLORATION AND APPLICATION	15 to 25	☐ *Option 1:* **ASK ME**—Solve puzzles, examine the eagerness of the Bereans in Acts 17:11, and discuss how we can find help in the Bible for our daily lives.	Puzzles with 25 to 50 pieces
	25 to 30	☐ *Option 2:* **EMBRACING WISDOM**—Explore Psalm 19:7-11; Proverbs 2:1-6; and 2 Timothy 3:16-17 to see what the Bible says about gaining wisdom from God's Word.	Bibles, poster board, markers, chalkboard
CLOSING	up to 10	**INSIGHTS**—Share biblical insights they've discovered in the past, read James 1:5, and pray together about group concerns.	Bibles, "Where to Find Help in the Bible" bookmarks (p.37)
FOR EXTRA TIME	up to 15	**THE SEARCH**—Ask questions to discover new things about others and compare that process to studying the Bible.	
	up to 10	**PROVERBIAL WISDOM**—Examine the wisdom in Proverbs 1–4.	Bibles
	up to 15	**FINDING HELP**—Use the "Where to Find Help in the Bible" handout to discover biblical insights on current concerns.	Bibles, "Where to Find Help in the Bible" bookmarks (p. 37)

Wisdom From Above

(up to 5 minutes)

As you begin the class, have volunteers tell what they discovered from their Bible study during the week.

Ask:

● **What did your study tell you about how Jesus approached the Scriptures?** (Jesus must've known the Old Testament well; he knew that God's Word goes deeper than laws and rules.)

● **What else did you learn about studying the Bible?** (It can be encouraging; it gives us wisdom.)

Say: **Last week we explored why it's important to study the Bible. Today, in the second week of our study on applying the Bible, we're going to explore how ▷ wisdom from the Bible is valuable in our lives.**

Open with prayer. Then encourage class members to get involved in the discussions and activities during the study.

BIBLE EXPLORATION AND APPLICATION

☐ OPTION 1:

Ask Me

(15 to 25 minutes)

Before this activity, you'll need to collect four or more different puzzles with 25 to 50 pieces each. Take pieces from each puzzle and mix them up in the other puzzles. For example, you might remove 10 pieces from one puzzle and place some of them in two or three of the other puzzles. Don't place pieces of one puzzle in *every* other puzzle—just some of them. When you're done, you should have puzzles that can only be completed if groups get pieces from each other.

Form at least four groups (a group can be one person). Give each group one of the mixed-up puzzles to put together as a team. Don't tell anyone that the puzzles have been mixed up.

People will soon discover that they have parts of other groups' puzzles and are missing some of their own. When this happens, tell groups they may send out members one at a time to ask for a puzzle piece from other groups. Adults must describe the kind of puzzle piece they want, but may not point to or pick up any puzzle piece. Based on their descriptions, the other group may give that person a puzzle piece.

Continue until all the puzzles are completed. Then have people discuss the following questions within their groups. After discussing each question, have volunteers share their groups' insights with the whole class.

Encourage a variety of responses before moving on.

Ask:

● **What was it like to discover you didn't have all the pieces of your puzzle?** (I expected that would happen; I didn't know where to go.)

● **How is that like the way you feel when you realize you don't have all the pieces for answering an important life question?** (In life, I get more concerned; I don't always know where to turn; my friends often have good ideas.)

● **How is the way you had to search in different places for puzzle pieces like the way we search the Bible for answers?** (Many Bible truths are scattered around in the Bible; it takes a lot of study to find what the Bible says about some topics.)

● **How is the way you received the puzzle piece you wanted like the way you uncover information in Bible study?** (Sometimes I get something I wasn't looking for when studying the Bible; I'm always excited to find a nugget of truth when studying the Bible.)

Have someone read Acts 17:11 aloud. Then ask the whole group:

● **What wisdom did the Bereans gain from examining the Scriptures?** (They knew who to believe; they learned what was right and what was wrong.)

● **How is our searching for answers in the Bible similar to the Bereans' examining of the Scriptures?** (We're both looking for truth; we try to find things to help us make decisions.)

● **Why do you think the Bereans were eager to examine the Scriptures?** (They knew they'd find the truth; they wanted to know if what they were hearing was right.)

● **How does our eagerness to study the Scriptures compare to the Bereans' eagerness?** (We tend to ignore the Bible most of the time; we aren't as eager, it's more like an obligation.)

● **How can we be more like the Bereans in our outlook on the Bible?** (We can make the Bible more important in our lives; we can study it more; we can depend on the Bible to help us make decisions.)

Say: **The Bible can be a powerful source for answers to our pressing questions and daily problems—if we use it.** ▶ **God's Word provides wisdom that's valuable in our lives.**

BIBLE INSIGHT

Luke, the author of Acts, says the Bereans were "of more noble character" than the Thessalonian Jews who had driven Paul and Silas away because of jealousy. Luke probably meant that the Berean Jews were more sincere followers of God than most Jews. They apparently lived by the true spirit of the Old Testament rather than the letter of the law, as many Jews did. The Berean Jews were not out to protect any religious system, but were seeking the truth as God revealed it to them.

◀ **THE POINT**

FOR *Even Deeper*
DISCUSSION

Form groups of no more than four and discuss the following questions:

● Why do many Christians spend more time reading the newspaper than the Bible?

● How much time should a Christian spend in personal Bible study each week? Why is it so hard to spend that much time? How can we overcome the obstacles to consistent personal Bible study?

■ ■

☐ **OPTION 2:**

Embracing Wisdom

(25 to 35 minutes)

Say: **We all face questions from time to time and need wisdom to answer them. Let's have a little fun finding out what some of those questions are.**

Form trios. Have people choose each member of their trio to be either the Question Mark, the Comma, or the Exclamation Point. Have trio members take turns sharing questions they've struggled with in recent weeks or months. Begin with the Question Mark, and announce when it's time for the Commas or Exclamation Points to talk. Allow no more than two minutes for each person.

Tell people they can talk about questions from any aspect of life such as work, home, relatives, or church. Questions might range from "Why did my father have to suffer so much before he died?" to "What should I do to find a new job?"

When six minutes are up, have people remain in their trios but let a volunteer from each trio tell the class about at least one question. Then have trios discuss the following questions. Ask:

● **What are the characteristics of a difficult question?** (We haven't dealt with it before; we don't have a source for finding the answer.)

● **When do you turn to the Bible for answers to your questions?** (When I can't find answers elsewhere; I look there first.)

Now have all the Question Marks gather in one place, the Commas in another place, and the Exclamation Points in a third place. Have these new groups choose a reader to read the assigned passage, a discussion leader to direct the discussion and make sure each person contributes ideas, a questioner(s) to ask questions that challenge people's conclusions and encourage critical thinking, and an artist to "draw" conclusions on poster board and report them to the class.

TEACHER

If you have fewer than 12 people in your class, have some people double up on roles in the new groups. If you have more than 20 people, have each new group divide into two groups, both studying the same passage.

Then assign the following passages: Question Marks—Psalm 19:7-11; Commas—Proverbs 2:1-6; and Exclamation Points—2 Timothy 3:16-17.

Give each group a piece of poster board and markers. Write the following questions on a chalkboard or newsprint. Say: **During the next 10 minutes, explore your assigned passage. As you discuss the verses, answer these questions:**

● **What does this passage say about Bible study?**

● **What does this passage tell us about finding answers in the Bible?**

● **What does this passage teach us about how we should approach Bible study?**

As groups explore their passages, roam from group to group and share any helpful information from the Bible Basis or Bible Insights in this lesson. Have the artists in each group use the poster board to illustrate symbolically their groups' findings. Encourage groups to help the artists come up with pictures and words to summarize the answers to the above questions.

After about 10 minutes, have artists present their posters and summarize the discussion. Then have people return to their original trios to discuss the following questions from the viewpoint of the passages they studied.

Ask:

● **How did your passage change the way you look at the Bible?** (I can trust the Bible to guide me to truth; I can look in the Bible for answers to my questions.)

● **How can we benefit from the wisdom in God's Word?** (By knowing what to do; by applying it to our daily lives.)

● **What kinds of questions might we have a difficult time finding answers to in the Bible?** (Questions about personal decisions; things like political correctness.)

Bring the class back together and read aloud John 16:12-15. Then ask:

● **What is the Holy Spirit's role in our study of the Bible?** (He helps us understand it; he teaches us what applies to our lives.)

● **How is the way our artists explained their posters like the way the Holy Spirit explains things in the Bible?** (He helps us understand things we wouldn't know otherwise; the Holy Spirit can explain the Bible best because he's the author, just like our artist was best at explaining the symbols since she created them.)

Say: ◆ **The wisdom in the Bible can be valuable in our lives. And with the Holy Spirit's guidance, we can better understand and apply the wisdom we find.**

BIBLE INSIGHT

In Psalm 19:7, the phrase "making wise the simple," carries a much deeper meaning than an English translation can provide. It indicates that the person who is easily led astray will be strengthened and will develop a solid, stable basis for living. God's Word will give meaning to the lives of us simple, easily deceived human beings.

The word "perfect" in Psalm 19:7 doesn't just mean "without fault." It also includes the idea of being absolutely positive in intent, totally directed toward the good of humans. God's Word will "revive the soul"—bringing a new, fresh life to anyone who believes it and lives by it.

TEACHER TIP

If a group feels "artistically challenged," encourage its members to come up with another creative way to illustrate their findings—such as through a skit, a song, or a creative presentation.

◀ **THE POINT**

■■■■■■■■■■■■■■■■■■■■■■■■■■■■■■■

FOR *Even Deeper* DISCUSSION

Form groups of no more than four and discuss the following questions:

● What's the relationship between the wisdom found in the Bible and the wisdom found in sources outside the Bible?

● How should we respond when something from science disagrees with the Bible? something from archaeology? something from psychology?

● How should we respond if we realize that *we* disagree with something in the Bible?

■■■■■■■■■■■■■■■■■■■■■■■■■■■■■■■

APPLY▪IT▪TO LIFE THIS WEEK

The "Apply-It-To-Life This Week" handout helps people further explore the issues uncovered in today's class. Give people copies of the handout (p. 38) before they leave and encourage them to take time during the coming week to explore the questions and activities listed on the handout.

CLOSING

Insights

(up to 10 minutes)

Form trios. If your class is already in trios from the previous activity, let them remain in the same trios. Have people tell their trio members about insights they've gained while studying the Bible. Encourage everyone to describe what it was like to uncover a relevant spiritual truth.

Have volunteers share their group members' insights with the class. Then read aloud James 1:5.

THE POINT ▷

Say: **The Bible says God will give us wisdom when we ask for it. And ▷ when we study the Bible we often discover the wisdom we need. Here's a handout that'll help us find biblical wisdom when we need it.**

Distribute copies of the "Where to Find Help in the Bible" bookmark (p.37) and give people a minute to look it over. Distribute several pairs of scissors to allow people to cut out their bookmarks. Then say: **Keep this bookmark in your Bible or another handy place. Refer to it when you need to find help for a specific concern you face.**

As we study our Bibles, we'll come across truths that help us live our lives for Christ more effectively. When the Holy Spirit leads us to a nugget of truth that applies to our lives, we'll benefit most by sharing that truth with

a friend. Let's make it our goal this week to share a Bible study insight with at least one other person.

Have trios pair up with other trios to make groups of six. Give these groups a few minutes to share prayer concerns. Then have volunteers in each group wrap up the study with prayer. Remind everyone to ask for God's help in sharing an insight from Scripture with someone this week.

For Extra Time

THE SEARCH
(up to 15 minutes)

Have people form trios, then say: **In your trios, ask each other any question you'd like. Find out things you don't already know about your group members. If you feel uncomfortable answering a question, you don't have to answer.**

Allow about five minutes for questions. If trios have trouble getting started, suggest a topic such as careers, dreams, or fears. Then discuss the following questions.

Ask:

● **How did you feel about the answers you received to your questions? Explain.**

● **What did you discover by asking questions?**

● **How does the way you searched for information about each other compare with the way we search for answers in the Bible?**

● **What can we learn about studying the Bible from this activity?**

PROVERBIAL WISDOM
(up to 10 minutes)

Form groups of four. Have groups assign one of the chapters from Proverbs 1–4 to each group member. Then have people discuss the chapters using the following questions to guide their discussion.

● **What's so valuable about wisdom?**

● **How does the wisdom mentioned in these chapters relate to the content of the Bible?**

● **What key things can we learn about wisdom from these chapters?**

FINDING HELP
(up to 15 minutes)

Form groups of four, and have participants share concerns they'd like to find biblical help with. Using their own Bible knowledge and the "Where to Find Help in the Bible" bookmark, have groups find passages that address the concerns they're facing. Have them use the following questions to help guide their discussions:

● **How does the message of this passage relate to the concern we're addressing?**

● **How can this passage of Scripture help in the situation?**

● **In light of this passage, what should our response be to the concern we're discussing?**

Where to Find Help in the Bible

Cut on solid outside line and fold on dotted line to make a bookmark.

To find help with:	Read:
Anger	Psalm 4:4 Psalm 37:7-11 Proverbs 29:11 Ephesians 4:26-32 James 1:19-20
Betrayal	Psalm 89:20-33 Hebrews 4:14-5:2
Bitterness	1 Corinthians 13 Ephesians 4:29–5:2 Hebrews 12:14-15 James 3:13-18
Confusion	Psalm 37:23-24 Psalm 143:8 Proverbs 3:5-6 James 3:16-18
Discouragement	Joshua 1:9 Psalm 77:6-15 Isaiah 35:3-10 2 Corinthians 4:16-18
Fear	Exodus 14:13-14 Deuteronomy 20:1-4 Joshua 1:9 Matthew 28:20 John 14:1-4; 25-27
Feeling unloved	Psalm 103: 8-18 Jeremiah 31:3-4 Hosea 14:4-6 Romans 8:35-39
Financial pressures	Luke 12:22-34 John 6:35 2 Corinthians 9:6-11 Philippians 4:19
Forgiveness	Psalm 32 Psalm 51 Luke 15:3-7 1 John 1:9
God's guidance	Proverbs 3:5-6 Luke 11:9-13 Ephesians 5:15-17 James 1:5-8
Guilty feelings	Psalm 51 Micah 7:18-19 Romans 8:1-4 Hebrews 10:16-23 1 John 1:9

To find help with:	Read:
Hurts	Psalm 34:17-19 John 14:1-4, 25-27 Revelation 7:13-17
Loneliness	Psalm 27:9-10 Psalm 146:5-10 John 16:31-33 Hebrews 13:5-6
Peace and rest	Psalm 62 Matthew 11:28-30 John 14:25-27 Philippians 4:6-9
Revenge	Matthew 5:38-42 Romans 12:14-21 1 Thessalonians 5:12-15 2 Thessalonians 1:6-9
Sadness	Psalm 23 Psalm 42 John 16:20-22 2 Corinthians 1:3-7 2 Thessalonians 2:16-17
Self-image	Genesis 1:26-31 Romans 5:6-8 1 Corinthians 12:12-18 1 John 3:1-3
Suffering	Romans 5:1-5 2 Corinthians 1:3-10 1 Peter 3:8-17 1 Peter 4:12-19
Temptation	1 Corinthians 10:13 2 Corinthians 10:3-5 Galatians 5:16-17 2 Thessalonians 3:3 Hebrews 4:15-16 1 Peter 5:8-10
Weakness	2 Corinthians 12:7-10 2 Thessalonians 3:2-3 1 Peter 5:8-10
Worry	Matthew 6:25-34 Philippians 4:4-7 1 Peter 5:6-7

From Group's Apply-It-To-Life™
Adult Bible Curriculum
Copyright © Group Publishing, Inc.

Our Questions, God's Answers

The Point: ▷ Wisdom from the Bible is valuable in our lives.

Scripture Focus: Psalm 19:7-11; Proverbs 2:1-6; Acts 17:11-12; and
2 Timothy 3:16-17

Reflecting on God's Word

Each day this week, read one of the following Scriptures and think about its relevance for today. Pray for guidance as you seek wisdom in God's Word. List your discoveries in the space under each reference.

Day 1: Matthew 10:16-20. Jesus sends out the disciples.

Day 2: Matthew 13:10-17. Jesus explains why he speaks in parables.

Day 3: Proverbs 8. Wisdom is personified.

Day 4: John 3:1-21. Jesus meets with Nicodemus.

Day 5: Philippians 2:1-16. Paul describes humility.

Day 6: 1 Peter 1:3-9. Peter praises God for hope in the face of suffering.

Beyond Reflection

1. After reading and thinking about one of the passages above, discover what Bible scholars have written about it. Use any resources you have, or go to your church library and look up the passages in Bible commentaries. Then compare what you saw in the passage with what you found in the commentaries. What new insights can you gain from others' interpretations?

2. Choose any Bible book and read through it, praying for the Holy Spirit's guidance. Take notes as you go along and put together an outline of the book. Determine what you think is the book's overall message. Watch for insights you've never thought of before. Then talk about your discoveries with a friend or family member. Discuss how your findings may affect your life.

Next Week's Bible Passages: 1 John 4:19-21 and Luke 11:37-54

A Relationship Blueprint

The Bible provides a blueprint for relationships with other people and with God.

◀ **THE POINT**

OBJECTIVES

Participants will
- explore what the Bible says about relationships,
- discover how relationships with people mirror relationships with God, and
- determine biblically based ways to grow in their relationships.

BIBLE BASIS

Read the Scripture for this lesson. Then read the following background paragraphs to see how the passage relates to people today.

In **1 John 4:19-21,** John states that someone can't hate his brother and love God at the same time.

In this passage and the preceding verses, John describes how all genuine love actually flows from God. People show God's love through their relationships. He reminds us that our relationships with others must mirror what we want our relationship with God to be. If we want a thriving relationship with God, we must have appropriate relationships with people.

John speaks boldly and sternly in this passage, expanding on a theme he's already discussed in this book (1 John 2:3-5; 3:16-18, 21-23; 4:7-12). In fact, his message is based on what Jesus himself said in John 15:10-12. John essentially says: "If we really love God, we'll act lovingly toward our Christian brothers and sisters. And if we don't act lovingly toward our

1 JOHN 4:19-21

Christian brothers and sisters, we don't really love God—no matter what we say." John isn't saying that a person who doesn't love another Christian *is incapable* of loving God, but that a lack of love proves the person *doesn't* love God.

If taken seriously, this passage would eliminate a lot of skirmishes among Christians; no longer would anyone hurt or wrong other Christians under the premise of "obeying God." This passage should also make us think about the message we send about our relationship with God when we fail to act lovingly toward others.

LUKE 11:37-54

In **Luke 11:37-54,** Jesus rebukes the Pharisees for wrong teaching.

In this passage, Jesus points out the danger of reducing our relationship with God to a list of rules or laws. Jesus' message to the Pharisees was to not ignore the law, but to stop defining their relationship with God in terms of their outward "spiritual" activities.

The incident that appears to have set off Jesus' scathing denunciation of the Pharisees was his failure to wash his hands and the resulting horror of the Pharisee. Note that the issue was not one of cleanliness; the problem was that the Pharisees demanded ritual hand-washing prior to a meal. The Old Testament Scriptures didn't demand the washing, but the Pharisees did.

Jesus' first statement must have startled the Pharisee, and it clearly introduced what Jesus was about to say: You're so worried about outer appearances and actions, but your hearts are selfish and wicked—not concerned about truly pleasing God.

Throughout this passage, Jesus indicts the Pharisees and experts in the law on relationship issues. They didn't take care of the poor (Luke 11:41); they ignored true justice (Luke 11:42); they didn't show God's love (Luke 11:42); they enjoyed looking more important than other people (Luke 11:43); they added to people's burdens (Luke 11:46); they didn't help those who were struggling (Luke 11:46); they persecuted and killed God's messengers (Luke 11:47-50); they weren't really pleasing God themselves (Luke 11:52); and they hindered those who truly sought to follow God (Luke 11:52). Instead of admitting that Jesus was right and seeking God's forgiveness, the Pharisees and teachers of the law opposed Jesus all the more.

Like the Pharisees, we can find ourselves basing our relationships on "do's" and "don'ts" instead of kindness and love. But this passage reminds us that God is more concerned about relationships than rules and regulations. When we explore the Bible to find God's blueprint for rela-tionships, we can discover insights that will make our relationships more pleasing to God today.

The Bible indicates that our relationship with God is closely connected to our relationships with people. As we seek to make our human relationships more pleasing to God, our relationship with him grows as well. We win all the way around!

Section	Minutes	What Participants Will Do	Supplies
OPENING	*up to 10*	**POSITIVE RELATIONSHIPS**—Learn about today's lesson and share stories of positive relationships.	
BIBLE EXPLORATION AND APPLICATION	*20 to 25*	☐ *Option 1:* **HOW DO WE RELATE?**—Respond to fictional relationship situations, and study what Luke 11:37-54 can tell us about how God wants us to relate to others.	"Relationship Stories" hand-outs (p. 48), pencils
	25 to 30	☐ *Option 2:* **RELATIONSHIP QUESTIONS**—Use various Scripture passages to develop biblical answers to relationship questions and to evaluate their own relationships.	Bibles, "Really Relating" hand-outs (p. 49), Bible study resources, pencils
CLOSING	*up to 10*	**APPRECIATED PEOPLE**—Share biblical relationship truths they've learned and express appreciation for other class members.	
FOR EXTRA TIME	*up to 10*	**THE BEST OF TIMES**—Discuss positive times in their relationships with God.	
	up to 15	**TOUGH SITUATIONS**—Discuss difficult relationship situations they're facing and suggest ways to deal with the situations.	
	up to 5	**BLUEPRINTS**—Compile a list of biblical insights to guide their relationships.	Bibles, pencils, paper

Positive Relationships

(up to 10 minutes)

As you begin the class, ask:

● **What did your study this week tell you about the wisdom found within the Bible?**

After several people respond, open with prayer. Encourage class members to get involved in the discussions and activities during the study.

Then tell everyone what you'll be learning in today's lesson. Say: **Welcome to our third week on why the Bible is relevant today. This week we're going to look at how the Bible is a guide for our relationships.**

Form groups of no more than four. Have each person take one minute to tell about a positive relationship and explain why that relationship is or was positive. For example, someone might tell about a friend who's always willing to listen. Let groups know when each minute has passed.

After all class members have shared, ask the following questions to the groups one question at a time. Have each person in each group answer every question. Ask:

● **What are the common factors in your positive relationship stories?** (The relationships were with close friends; the other person was willing to listen.)

● **What are the common factors of a relationship that isn't working?** (People don't communicate; people don't care about each other.)

● **How do we learn to relate to other people?** (From our parents; from those we work with.)

● **What are the most difficult relationship issues you've faced?** Answers will vary.

Say: **Our interactions with family, friends, and people we don't know often cause stress in our lives. Relationships are at the core of who we are and what we do. But where do we go to find out what our relationships should or could be?** ▶ **The Bible provides a blueprint for our relationships with other people and with God. Today we're going to explore what the Bible has to say about relationships.**

THE POINT ▷

BIBLE EXPLORATION AND APPLICATION

☐ **OPTION 1:**

How Do We Relate?

(20 to 30 minutes)

Form groups of about four people and distribute a "Relationship Stories" handout (p. 48) to each group. If you have fewer than six class members, stay in one group and discuss as many of the "Relationship Stories" as time permits.

Each group will be a "relationship task force." Assign one relationship story to each task force and have people discuss their situation and the questions that follow.

Ask task forces to brainstorm specific things each person in the situation should do to resolve the negative aspects of the situation. Have task force members work to find solutions they all agree on, but encourage people to be honest if they disagree. Have them prepare to report only the conclusions that their task force members all agree on.

Allow plenty of time for discussion. Then have task forces summarize their situations for the class and present only those ideas the whole group agrees upon. Allow the task forces to stay seated together.

Then ask the whole group:

● **How easy was it to agree on solutions to these problems?** (Not very easy; they seemed pretty clear to us.)

● **What was it like to relate in your task force as you attempted to come to a consensus?** (We worked well together; we didn't agree much.)

● **How is the way you worked toward a solution like the way people relate in everyday life?** (People don't always agree, but can they can compromise; people do their best to work together.)

● **What does this activity tell us about relationships?** (Relationships are tough; it's a challenge to work things out together.)

Say: **The Bible has a lot to say about positive and negative relationships. Let's take a look at a negative example that Jesus pointed out.**

Have someone in each task force read Luke 11:37-54 aloud. Then have task forces discuss the following questions within their groups:

● **What was wrong with the way the Pharisees and experts in the law had been handling relationships?** (They had been too worried about their rules and not about people; they had neglected the poor and cared only about their own status.)

● **How were the Pharisees' actions similar to the actions of your task force members? How were they different?** (We struggled with being fair to everyone; we all wanted our own ideas to be chosen; we had a lot more love than the Pharisees; we didn't even talk about what the Bible might say.)

● **What does this passage tell us about God's outlook on our relationships with others?** (It indicates that God is more concerned about people being treated fairly than about every little rule being followed; it shows that he cares about relationships and how we act toward others.)

● **What does this passage tell us about what our relationship with God should be like?** (We need to be sincere; we can't be selfish; God wants our love more than our blind traditional practices.)

After the task forces have discussed the questions, have them report highlights of their discussions to the whole class. Then say: **We can look in a lot of different places for ways to handle our relationships with other people. But we need to remember that the Bible is a great source for help in our relationships. In many ways, ▶ the Bible is a blueprint for relationships, both with other people and with God.**

THE POINT▶

■■■■■■■■■■■■■■■■■■■■■■■■■■■■■■■■

FOR *Even Deeper* DISCUSSION   Form groups of no more than four and discuss the following questions:

● Who might be considered "Pharisees" today when it comes to relationships? What would Jesus say to today's "Pharisees"?

● What does Jesus' confrontation of the Pharisees tell us about relationships? Should we ever respond like Jesus did? Why or why not?

● What relationship situations do we really face today in which we need help? How can the Bible help in those situations?

■■■■■■■■■■■■■■■■■■■■■■■■■■■■■■■■

☐ **OPTION 2:**
Relationship Questions
(25 to 35 minutes)

Have people form groups of four. If you used Option 1, adults may stay in their task force groups. Within each group have participants fill the following roles: reader (to read the passages aloud), recorder (to record notes about the passages), reporter (to report the group's findings to the rest of the class), and researcher (to explore what the Bible says about the group's question).

Give each person a copy of the "Really Relating" handout and assign each group a relationship question from the handout. Make available whatever Bible study resources you can, such as study Bibles, concordances, and Bible commentaries.

Say: **Do your best to find a biblical answer to your assigned question. Use the passages and the infor-**

mation you've been given on the handout, but also refer to any other passages you can find that relate to your question. Also discuss information you find in these Bible study resources.

After about 15 minutes, call groups together. It's OK if groups haven't formulated clear answers to their question. Have reporters read their questions to the class and summarize the conclusions they made based on their biblical discoveries.

Then ask:

● **What general principles can we draw from these passages to guide our relationships with other people?** (We should always be loving; we need to be kind even to people who don't like us.)

Encourage people to keep thinking until they've come up with several good principles. Then ask:

● **What principles can we draw from these passages to guide our relationship with God?** (When we're kind to people, we're pleasing God; a good relationship with God will result in our treating others properly.)

Again, encourage people to keep thinking until they've given several answers. Then ask:

● **How is the Bible like a blueprint for relationships?** (There are lots of different things to look at; it shows us how we should live; when we figure out what it says, we learn how to relate to others.)

Say: **We've discussed how the Bible can help guide our relationships; now let's see how each of us is applying the truths we've discovered.**

Ask:

● **What have you discovered today that makes you feel good about your relationships?** (I like to serve other people; I enjoy listening to others.)

● **What have you discovered today that you'd like to change about your relationships?** (I've often been too afraid to lovingly confront a friend; I think I sometimes expect too much from others.)

● **What does the quality of your relationships with others say about the quality of your relationship with God?** (We treat God the same way we treat others; I have a hard time letting God love me, just as I have a hard time letting other people love me.)

Say: ▶ **The Bible really is like a blueprint for relationships. It provides the guidelines we need to build solid, meaningful relationships with people and with God. Just like a contractor studies a blueprint to understand what to do on a construction project, we need to study the Bible to understand what to do in our relationships with others and with God.**

BIBLE
INSIGHT

In Luke 6:27, Jesus tells us to love our enemies. He's not just referring to people we oppose in some way, but to anyone who might have hostile feelings toward us—for whatever reason. We are to show love to them even if they never respond. And the love Jesus talks about isn't a warm, fuzzy feeling, but an attitude of service and a desire to do good things for the other person.

In Galatians 6:1, the Greek word translated "restore" indicates bringing something back to its original condition. This same word was used to describe the mending of fishing nets and the setting of broken bones. When Paul tells us in Galatians 6:2 to "carry each other's burdens," he's saying that we should support and encourage each other any way we can. In that way we're doing what Christ wants us to do—loving each other as he has loved us (John 15:12).

In Matthew 25:35-36, Jesus lists actions that demonstrate a person's faith—actions that he says we do for him when we do them for others in need. Notice that none of these actions are tremendously difficult. He doesn't mention buying someone a house or risking our lives. Instead, he mentions giving a hot meal, a glass of water, a warm welcome, a change of clothes, caring for a sick person, and visiting a prisoner. By mentioning the little things, Jesus points out their importance. If we neglect to do them for each other, we're neglecting our relationship with him.

◀ T H E   P O I N T

■■■■■■■■■■■■■■■■■■■■■■■■■■■■

FOR *Even Deeper*
DISCUSSION

Form groups of no more than four and discuss the following questions:

● Read Luke 15:11-32. What can we learn about relationships from the actions of the father? the younger son? the older son?

● What does it really mean to love your enemies? Who are our "enemies"? How can we show love to those people?

● Read Matthew 12:46-50. How do Jesus' actions and words in this passage relate to family relationships? church relationships?

■■■■■■■■■■■■■■■■■■■■■■■■■■■■

 The "Apply-It-To-Life This Week" handout helps people further explore the issues uncovered in today's class. Give people the handout (p. 50) before they leave and encourage them to take time during the coming week to explore the questions and activities.

CLOSING

Appreciated People

(up to 10 minutes)

Form a circle. Then have each person share a simple biblical truth about relationships that he or she learned or was reminded of in today's class. Encourage people to keep their insights brief. After each person speaks, have the person on his or her right express appreciation for that person, mentioning thoughts from class, from personal lives, or from the insights the person shared. Let affirmations continue to the left until everyone has spoken and received appreciation.

 THE POINT ▷

Then say: **Let's pray together,** ▷ **thanking God for the Bible's blueprint for relationships.**

Wrap up your class by allowing volunteers to pray. Then thank people for attending and encourage them to continue studying the Bible during the week using the "Apply-It-To-Life This Week" handout.

For Extra Time

THE BEST OF TIMES
(up to 10 minutes)

Form pairs. Have partners take turns completing the following statement: **One time I really felt good about my relationship with God was . . .**

Then have partners discuss the following questions:

● **What's the most difficult thing about your relationship with God? with other people?**

● **How do you know when your relationship with God is good? when it's bad?**

● **What helps you maintain good relationships with people? with God?**

Allow a few minutes for discussion, then have volunteers share their insights with the whole group.

TOUGH SITUATIONS
(up to 5 minutes)

Form groups of no more than four and have people list difficult relationship situations they've faced or are facing. Then have groups discuss the situations and explore ways to deal with those kinds of relationships. Encourage people to apply the biblical principles they've just learned. After a few minutes of discussion, have group members pray together for the people who've been mentioned.

BLUEPRINTS
(up to 5 minutes)

Give adults paper and pencils and have them create "blueprints" for relationships by listing biblical insights from today's class. Encourage people to keep these blueprints and add to them as they study the Bible and discover other relationship guidelines.

RELATIONSHIP STORIES

SITUATION 1:

Sam confides in Sarah, his associate, that he and his wife are having marital trouble. Sam is truly upset by his family situation and needs someone to help him sort it out. Sarah, who's always been attracted to Sam, wants to help. She suggests that Sam go out to dinner with her so they can talk. Sam's wife calls and asks when he'll be home.

What are the relationship "crisis points" in this situation?
What should Sam do?
What should Sarah do?
What are the potential areas for relationship problems?
How does each person's response to this situation reflect his or her other relationships?

SITUATION 2:

Bonnie and Liz haven't been talking for the past three weeks because Liz told another friend that Bonnie hadn't *quit* her previous job—she'd been *fired* for talking back to her boss. Though what Liz said was true, Bonnie didn't appreciate having Liz—her best friend—share the information with someone else. Liz contends that she told the other friend about the firing to correct the worse things that friend had heard about Bonnie's lack of employment.

What are the relationship "crisis points" in this situation?
What should Bonnie do?
What should Liz do?
What are the potential areas for relationship problems?
How does each person's response to this situation reflect his or her other relationships?

SITUATION 3:

Gary's mother, Elizabeth, is 78 years old and has been living alone for 17 years. She still gets around OK, but recently she's had near disasters such as forgetting to turn off the stove and not remembering what she did with large sums of money. Gary feels that he should put his mother in some type of elder-care facility, but he's an only child and the financial burden would be heavy. Denise, Gary's wife, is willing to help care for Elizabeth in their home, but the time involvement and the disruption of family life would be hard on her and their two teenagers. Elizabeth is resistant to any change, insisting that she can still take care of herself.

What are the relationship "crisis points" in this situation?
What should Gary do?
What should Denise do?
What are the potential areas for relationship problems?
How does each person's response to this situation reflect his or her other relationships?

■ REALLY RELATING

Within your group, develop a biblical answer to your assigned question. Use the passages and information given with your question, other passages that relate to the question, and any other Bible study resources available.

---

1. **How should I relate to people I don't get along with?**
(Luke 6:27-36; Romans 12:17-21)

F.Y.I. In Luke 6:27, Jesus tells us to love our enemies. He's not just referring to people we oppose in some way, but to anyone who might have hostile feelings toward us—for whatever reason. We are to show love to them even if they never respond. And the love Jesus talks about isn't a warm, fuzzy feeling, but an attitude of service and a desire to do good things for the other person.

---

2. **What responsibility do I have to work on healing damaged relationships?**
(Galatians 6:1-6; 1 Thessalonians 5:14-15)

F.Y.I. In Galatians 6:1, the Greek word translated "restore" indicates bringing something back to its original condition. This same word was used to describe the mending of fishing nets and the setting of broken bones. When Paul tells us in Galatians 6:2 to "carry each other's burdens," he's saying we should support and encourage each other any way we can. In that way we're doing what Christ wants us to do—loving each other as he has loved us (John 15:12).

---

3. **What does the way I relate to others say about how I relate to God?**
(1 John 4:19-21; Matthew 25:31-46)

F.Y.I. In Matthew 25:35-36, Jesus lists actions that demonstrate a person's faith—actions he says we do for him when we do them for others in need. Notice that none of these actions are tremendously difficult. He doesn't mention buying someone a house or risking our lives. Instead, he mentions giving a hot meal, a glass of water, a warm welcome, a change of clothes, caring for a sick person, and visiting a prisoner. By mentioning the little things, Jesus points out their importance. If we neglect to do them for each other, we're neglecting our relationship with him.

A Relationship Blueprint

The Point: ▶ The Bible provides a blueprint for our relationships with other people and with God.

Scripture Focus: 1 John 4:19-21 and Luke 11:37-54

Reflecting on God's Word

Each day this week, read one of the following Scriptures and examine what that passage says about relationships. List your discoveries in the space under each passage.

Day 1: Philippians 2:1-4. Consider others better than ourselves.

Day 2: Romans 12:9-21. Love others through your actions.

Day 3: 1 John 3:11-15. If we love God, we'll love fellow believers.

Day 4: 1 Corinthians 8:13. Be careful to not lead others toward sin.

Day 5: Hebrews 13:1-3. Care for strangers and prisoners.

Day 6: Proverbs 15:18. Be patient, not hot tempered.

Beyond Reflection

1. Discuss the following questions with a friend:
● What makes it difficult to express negative feelings toward God?
● How does the way we're honest or dishonest with other people about our feelings reflect how we relate to God?
● What is a healthy way to express negative thoughts or feelings to friends? to strangers? to God?

2. Begin a study of how Jesus related to his disciples. Read the book of Mark and write down every interaction you find between Jesus and the disciples. Then synthesize your observations to come up with Jesus' theology of relationships. Compare this to your own and see where you might improve to become more Christlike. Be prepared for a surprise, however; Jesus wasn't afraid of speaking the truth or of experiencing pain in relationship with others.

Next Week's Bible Passage: 1 Peter

Exploring the Bible in Context

If we study the context of a Bible passage, we can better understand and apply the passage.

O B J E C T I V E S

Participants will
- learn the importance of understanding context,
- explore the context of Bible books, and
- be encouraged to apply biblical truths to their lives.

B I B L E   B A S I S

Read the Scripture for this lesson. Then read the following background paragraphs to see how the passage relates to people today.

1 Peter was written to address the issue of suffering in the early church.

This short Bible book includes several familiar passages that we may pull out to use for particular situations, such as "Cast all your anxiety on him because he cares for you" (1 Peter 5:7, New International Version). That passage can be a great comfort to someone who is anxious or worried.

But upon exploration of the "why" behind the book, we discover valuable information that gives that verse even more meaning. We find that Peter's whole message addresses the issue of suffering and persecution. In fact, in the New International Version of this short five-chapter book, Peter uses some form of the word "suffer" 18 times. He mentions it at least twice in every chapter.

Peter doesn't tell us the details of the suffering, but it appears to be related to persecution for following Christ. Peter may have written this book around A. D. 65-66, during the reign of the Roman emperor Nero. In A. D. 64, devastating fires had raged through Rome, destroying over half the city. Some Romans at that time suspected that Nero instigated the fires in a plot to get rid of the older, poorer parts of the city and build a new, more glorious Rome.

To divert suspicion from himself, Nero accused the Christians of arson and began persecuting them. Anyone confessing to be a Christian was arrested, and many were tortuously executed. At Nero's direction, the Romans crucified some of the Christians, burned some as torches at night, and covered others with animal skins and then set wild dogs after them. Other Roman leaders likely followed Nero's example and began persecuting Christians throughout the Roman empire. Both Paul and Peter were probably executed by Nero during this time of persecution.

Throughout this book, Peter encourages his fellow Christians to continue being faithful in suffering for the sake of Christ. In 1 Peter 2:21 and 4:1, Peter reminds his readers that they are to follow Jesus' example of suffering. In 1 Peter 2:18-21, he encourages slaves to submit to good *and harsh* masters—and commends those who bear the pain of suffering. In 1 Peter 4:12-13, he tells his fellow Christians they shouldn't be surprised that they're suffering. And in 1 Peter 1:6 and 5:10, Peter indicates the suffering is only for a little while—possibly meaning that death will eventually end the suffering.

All of these passages mean more to us when we realize what the people Peter was addressing were going through. They weren't just facing teasing or discrimination because of their faith; they were facing death! As we explore the historical context of 1 Peter, we can begin to put our own suffering into a proper perspective. And the further we dig into Peter's writings, the more we learn about good and bad reasons for suffering, how we're to suffer, and the result of suffering. Peter's advice for those suffering during severe persecution can serve as a powerful guide for Christians living in post-Christian societies today.

What we learn through studying the context of 1 Peter is just one example of the new insights and relevance we can find when we explore biblical contexts. Our study is always enriched when we discover why a particular book or passage was written. Though pulling verses out of context to support our beliefs is tempting (and common), we can gain much more by understanding the bigger picture. We can uncover unique and relevant biblical truths when we seek to understand the "whys" behind a book or passage.

Section	Minutes	What Participants Will Do	Supplies
OPENING	*up to 10*	**WHAT'S RELEVANT?**—Learn about today's lesson and tell relevant and irrelevant statements about themselves.	Paper, pencils
BIBLE EXPLORATION AND APPLICATION	25 to 35	☐ *Option 1:* **OUT OF CONTEXT**—Discover how context is important for understanding and examine how the context of 1 Peter helps us better understand passages in the book.	Novels or biographies, Bibles,
	20 to 25	☐ *Option 2:* **ASKING THE RIGHT QUESTIONS**—Explore an entire Bible book to uncover the context and apply the central message of the book.	Bibles, Bible study resources, "Book Introductions" handouts (p.60), pencils, paper, newspapers, tape
CLOSING	*up to 5*	**GOOD WORDS**—Tell each other reasons they enjoyed studying together and pray together to wrap up the course.	
⏱ **FOR EXTRA TIME**	*up to 5*	**COURSE REFLECTION**—Examine and reflect on what they've gained from this course.	
	up to 10	**FAVORITE BOOKS**—Tell what their favorite Bible books are and why.	

What's Relevant?

(up to 10 minutes)

THE POINT ▷

As you begin the class, say: **Welcome to the final week of our study on why the Bible is relevant. Today we're going to explore how ▷ understanding the context of a Bible passage can bring new meaning and application for our lives.**

Open with prayer. Encourage class members to get involved in the discussions and activities during the study.

Distribute paper and pencils. Say: **On your paper, write four bits of information about yourself. Choose two items that might help someone know more about you. Then list two other bits of information that are true but not relevant in helping others get to know you.**

For relevant items, someone might write:

● I love to spend time outdoors.
● I bought a sports car last week.

Then that person could add irrelevant facts, such as:

● I go to work every day.
● I do laundry on Saturdays.

Allow everyone four minutes to make a list. Then form groups of no more than five. Have group members take turns reading their lists out loud, mixing up the relevant and irrelevant facts. Encourage adults to guess the items that are irrelevant in getting to know that person.

After a few minutes, ask the following questions and have groups discuss them:

● **How easy was it to guess the irrelevant statements? Explain.** (Some were easy because they stood out in people's lists; some weren't easy because they all seemed relevant.)

● **Were any of the statements truly irrelevant? Explain.** (No, everything told us something about the person; yes, we already knew he had two arms.)

● **How was this activity similar to your experience in studying the Bible?** (Some things that don't seem relevant at first become relevant when we think about them; sometimes it's hard to know what I'm supposed to do.)

● **How is it unlike your experience in studying the Bible?** (The Bible is harder to figure out; nothing in the Bible is irrelevant.)

Say: **Sometimes information is more relevant than it seems at first. And sometimes things in the Bible become more relevant as we study them more thoroughly. One thing that helps us see the relevancy of a Bible passage we're studying is to understand its context. When we study a passage in its context, we can better understand the passage and apply it to our lives.**

☐ OPTION 1:
Out of Context
(25 to 35 minutes)

Form groups of no more than four. Give each group a few novels or biographies. Say: **Spend the next six minutes scanning your books to find quotes that might have meaning for you today. Look for one- or two-sentence quotes that might address a situation someone in your group has faced.**

Allow about six minutes for groups to find quotes. Then have volunteers read their quotes for the whole class.

After each quote, ask:

● **Why is or isn't this a useful quote?** (It's useful because it speaks to a current need; it doesn't make sense out of context.)

● **What can you learn about the whole book from this quote?** (Nothing; a little bit about the plot; very little.)

After exploring all the quotes in this manner, ask class members the following questions. Encourage responses from at least three different people for each question.

Ask:

● **How might the quotes you read take on new meaning once you understood the context?** (They could mean the opposite of what we thought; we might gain a deeper understanding of the quote.)

● **How is this activity like or unlike the way people use the Bible?** (People often use verses out of context to support their beliefs; some verses out of context still say good things.)

● **What good result can come from looking at specific verses without the benefit of understanding context?** (Sometimes a single verse can be uplifting; God can use any part of the Bible to help someone; in the long run, I think it does more harm than good.)

● **How might exploring the context of specific verses help us gain deeper meaning from the passage?** (We might learn what the people were going through and better understand how the message applies; we might discover that the verse doesn't really say what we originally thought.)

Say: **God can use the Bible in many different ways. Sometimes a particular verse is just what we need to overcome a difficult situation or to experience joy during troubled times. ▶ But by exploring the context of a Bible passage, we can uncover relevant insights.**

◀ **THE POINT**

Right now we're going to take a look at an entire book of the Bible—1 Peter—and see how its context

affects the way we look at messages within it. We can learn a lot about the context of a book simply by reading it in its entirety. Or we can gain insights about the context of a book by looking it up in a study Bible or a Bible handbook. Right now let's see what we can discover from within the book itself.

Form groups of five and assign each group member one of the following passages: 1 Peter 1:1, 6-7; 1 Peter 2:19-21; 1 Peter 3:13-17; 1 Peter 4:12-16, 19; or 1 Peter 5:10, 12.

Have group members read their passages aloud, then have them discuss these questions within their groups. Ask:

● **What does your passage indicate about the people who received Peter's letter?** (They were suffering; they needed encouragement; they were being persecuted for their faith.)

● **What reasons do you see for the writing of the letter?** (To encourage people; to give hope; to reassure people that their faith was right.)

● **How do your insights into Peter's initial readers and his reasons for writing affect the way you look at other verses in 1 Peter?** (It helps me understand them better; it lets me know more about Peter.)

After groups have discussed all three questions, have them report their conclusions to the rest of the class. Then read aloud portions of the Bible Basis (p. 51) that you feel would be most helpful to your class.

Say: **Let's test what we've just been talking about. I'm going to read aloud some other verses from 1 Peter. Think about how you understand these verses differently because of what you know about the writer and the setting.**

Read each of the following passages aloud. After each one, have volunteers answer the question that follows the verses. Read 1 Peter 1:13-16; 3:8-9; 5:7; and 5:8-9.

● **How has your understanding of this passage changed, knowing what we've learned about the author and setting of 1 Peter?** Answers will vary with each passage.

After your discussion, ask the following question. Wait for several responses before moving on.

● **How will our examination of these passages in their context affect the way you live this week?** (I'll be a little more willing to tell others about my faith; I won't be so ready to complain when things go wrong.)

Say: **Peter spoke to people who were suffering because they were Christians. When we examine Peter's message in relation to its context, we learn more about what it means to suffer for our faith today.**

For *Even Deeper* DISCUSSION

Form groups of no more than four and discuss the following questions:

● How does our setting differ from what we know of the setting for 1 Peter? How is it the same? How do we suffer for Christ today?

● Read 1 Peter 3:15-16. What does this passage say to us today, since we know that the people Peter wrote this to were suffering for their faith? How can we show gentleness and respect when telling others about our faith in Jesus?

■ ■

□ OPTION 2:
Asking the Right Questions
(20 to 25 minutes)

Form groups of no more than four. Give each group a Bible, a study Bible or a Bible handbook, paper, and pencils. Assign one of the following books of the Bible to each group: Joel, Philemon, or 2 Peter.

TEACHER TIP

If you don't have study resources available, everyone can still refer to the "Book Introductions" handout.

BIBLE INSIGHT

For background information on Joel, Philemon, and 2 Peter, see the "Book Introductions" handout.

Say: **Now we're going to explore three Bible books to discover as much as possible about the authors' reasons for writing. We'll also look for questions or problems the authors were attempting to address.**

Then say: **Look through your assigned book for repeated phrases and references to specific problems. Use the resources you have to help find background information and make a list of clues that relate to why the author wrote the book. See if you can find answers to the following questions:**

● **What situation prompted the author to write this book?**

● **What problems does the author address?**

● **What solutions does the author suggest?**

Encourage people to dig into their research. Visit each group to help keep people on task. After about five minutes, give everyone a copy of the "Book Introductions" handout. After at least five more minutes, call everyone together and have volunteers share their groups' insights with the whole class.

Ask:

● **What did you learn by exploring the context of the book?** Answers will vary.

● **How is this approach to Bible study different from simply analyzing the words on the page?** (This way you get to know the situation better; the more you understand the context, the better chance you have of making a correct interpretation.)

Say: ▷ **Understanding the context of a Bible passage helps us gain new meaning for today. Let's take the next step and apply to our lives what we've discovered.**

Have groups brainstorm applications of the Bible books they studied. Encourage people to think of current situations that resemble those written about in the book.

Allow them about five minutes to do this, then hold up a recent newspaper. Say: **This newspaper represents our current context—what's happening around us.**

Have volunteers call out relevant applications of their book of the Bible one at a time. Each time someone gives a modern-day application (and the class agrees that it's a valid statement), tape a sheet of the newspaper to the wall. Continue until you've covered a good portion of one wall.

Ask:

● **What was it like to dig for relevant application from the context of a Bible book?** (It was difficult; some applications came easily.)

Then say: **A quick glance at the amount of newspaper on the wall tells us that the Bible is indeed relevant for today. As we end this course, let's each commit to dig deeply into the Bible for the relevant truths God has placed there for us.**

■ ■

FOR *Even Deeper* DISCUSSION

Form groups of no more than four and discuss the following questions:

● Can God speak through Bible verses even when they're taken out of context? Explain.

● Can Bible verses become damaging when taken out of context? Explain.

● How can we know if it's OK to use a Bible verse without using or explaining its context?

■ ■

APPLY■IT■TO LIFE THIS WEEK The "Apply-It-To-Life This Week" handout helps people further explore the issues uncovered in today's class. Give people copies of the handout (p. 61) before they leave and encourage them to take time during the coming week to explore the questions and activities listed on the handout.

Good Words

(up to 5 minutes)

Say: **Today we've explored how** ▷ **understanding the context of a Bible passage can help us uncover new meaning and application for today. We can learn a lot about the Bible when we study it together in groups, just as we've done these past four weeks.**

Encourage everyone to continue studying the Bible in small groups. Then have people mingle and tell at least three others one thing they appreciated about their contributions to the course. For example, someone might say, "I enjoyed your insightful comments today" or "Your openness to new ideas inspired me to 'think out of the box,' too."

Call everyone together in a circle to join hands in a closing prayer. Invite people to contribute to the prayer.

Ask people what they liked most about the course and what they'd like to see changed. Please note their comments (along with your own) and send them to the Adult Curriculum Editor at Group Publishing, Box 481, Loveland, Colorado, 80539. We want your feedback so that we can make each course better than the last. Thanks!

◁ **THE POINT**

 ## For Extra Time

COURSE REFLECTION

(up to 5 minutes)

Encourage adults to reflect on the past four lessons. Have them take turns completing the following sentences:
- Something I learned in this course was...
- If I could tell friends about this course, I'd say...
- Something I'll do differently because of this course is...

FAVORITE BOOKS

(up to 10 minutes)

Have each person turn to a partner to discuss the following questions:
- **What's your favorite book of the Bible?**
- **What makes this book meaningful to you?**
- **How do you apply the insights from this book to everyday life?**

Ask volunteers to share their partners' insights with the whole class.

■ BOOK INTRODUCTIONS

JOEL

● **Situation:** Locusts have just swept down on the land of Judah and devoured all the crops. The ground is stripped bare of vegetation, and the future looks bleak for the people, who depend on the crops to feed themselves and their livestock.

● **Problems:** The people of Judah have been ignoring the Lord, and the plague of locusts came as God's judgment for sin. If they continue in their ways and refuse to repent, the people will be judged even more harshly by God.

● **Solution:** Joel's solution (as prompted by God) is to encourage the people to repent and to return to God. He suggests two good reasons for doing that. First of all, if they don't repent and serve God, God may destroy them in judgment. Second, if they do repent and honor God with their lives, he will bless them abundantly. Joel also encourages the people in their suffering, pointing out that one day God will judge their enemies as well.

PHILEMON

● **Situation:** Paul knew both Onesimus [oh-NESS-eh-mas] and Philemon [fye-LEE-mun], who were both from Colosse [kuh-LOSS-ee]. Onesimus was a slave who had run away from his Christian master, Philemon. Onesimus had likely chosen to hide out in the big city of Rome so that slave hunters wouldn't find him. Now, Onesimus had become a Christian through Paul's ministry. Paul was in prison, and Onesimus had been helping care for his needs.

● **Problems:** Runaway slaves were in big trouble in the Roman Empire. Their masters had the right to have them put to death. On top of that, it appears that Onesimus may have stolen something from Philemon. Onesimus was now a Christian and wanted to do what was right, but was probably worried about retribution if he returned to Philemon.

● **Solution:** Paul wrote this letter to Philemon, encouraging him to forgive Onesimus and accept him back as a Christian brother. Paul had apparently helped Philemon become a Christian. Paul reminded him of that and encouraged Philemon to accept Onesimus as if Onesimus were Paul himself.

2 PETER

● **Situation:** Heretical teachings were springing up within the church. False teachers were saying there would be no judgment and were proclaiming a lifestyle of immorality and indulgence in all sorts of evil. Their teachings amounted to rebellion against God.

● **Problems:** False teachers were promoting their teachings within the churches, trying to convince the Christians that false beliefs were true Christianity. They were deceiving Christians and drawing them away from the truth.

● **Solution:** Peter writes to warn these early Christians to be true to Jesus and his teachings. He encourages them to grow and mature in their faith so they can be prepared to confront the false teachers. He reminds them that Jesus will return and he prods them to live pure, faithful lives as they wait.

Exploring the Bible in Context

APPLY■IT■TO
LIFE
THIS WEEK

The Point: ▶ If we study the context of a Bible passage, we can better understand and apply the passage.

Scripture Focus: 1 Peter

Reflecting on God's Word

Each day this week, read one of the following Bible passages and explore the context. Then apply the message of the passage to your own life. List your discoveries in the space under each reference.

Day 1: Psalm 64. David pleads for protection.

Day 2: Luke 4–6. Jesus heals and teaches.

Day 3: Jude. Jude condemns false teachers and calls for faithfulness.

Day 4: 1 John. John refutes false teachers and encourages Christians to love each other.

Day 5: Jonah. Jonah preaches God's message after running from God.

Day 6: 2 Timothy. Paul gives final instructions to Timothy.

Beyond Reflection

1. Choose one Bible book and study it without using any other resources. Make notes as you study to help you uncover the reason the book was written, the audience it was intended for, and the kinds of issues that were significant at the time. Once you've come up with several insights, compare what you discovered with what you find in Bible study resources. Or study the same Bible book that a friend is studying and compare conclusions.

2. Ask a pastor or another appropriate person for advice on Bible study resources. Borrow or buy resources to help you in your Bible study. Examine what the resources say about the context of a passage before you begin studying it. See what new insights grow out of the passage as you study.

3. Pray daily for a better understanding of Scripture.

Fellowship and Outreach Specials

Use the following activities any time you want. You can use them as part of—or in place of—your regular class activities, or you might consider planning a special event based on one or more of the ideas.

Study Bible Bible Study
Form groups of no more than four and have people commit to study a book of the Bible for at least six weeks. Encourage everyone to get a study Bible (the kind filled with margin notes and insights) and to learn how to use all of its features. If you have a budget for resources, consider purchasing one or more study Bibles for each study group to use. Encourage groups to share and pray about praises and concerns.

A Book a Month
Form a "book of the month club" and arrange to meet once a month. Have club members read a different book of the Bible each month, then come together to share insights, questions, and issues that came out of their reading. You might want to divide larger books (such as Psalms) into smaller sections to allow for more in-depth reading each month. Encourage participants to invite non-Christian friends.

Breakfast Bible Club
Start several same-gender Bible study/fellowship groups with people in your church. Some people may be able to meet for breakfast early in the morning before going to work; others may want to meet mid-morning or in the evening. Encourage people to work on building relationships and holding each other accountable to apply the Bible to their lives.

Bible to Life
Put one of the most significant messages of the Bible into action—serve others joyfully. Collect low-cost New Testaments ahead of time (by fund-raising efforts or donations), then head out in small groups to serve people in your community. Groups might help paint a house, clean a garage, fix a meal, or help with day care. Ask everyone to do this work for free and have them give a New Testament to those they helped. Adults might also want to invite the people they help to church.

Exploratory Bible Class

Have interested individuals prepare and lead basic Bible study groups for people in your church or community. Work with the volunteers to develop an interactive, experiential course that helps participants discover the richness of the Bible and its relevance for today. Someone might want to lead a class like this for your church's teenagers or older children. For resources, check out **Real Life Bible Curriculum, Active Bible Curriculum,** and other courses in **Apply-It-To-Life Adult Bible Curriculum** from Group Publishing.

Discovery Party

Encourage people to list their Bible study discoveries as they work on their Bible studies during each week. Then, once a quarter (or more often), meet to share in a "discovery" party. During the party, have people share the biblical discoveries they've made in the past weeks. Serve out-of-the-ordinary food so that each person can discover a new favorite. And play new games so everyone can discover new ways to interact and learn about each other.